"At times wry, sly, sober, Anthony Murphy conveys the extraordinary in the ordinary. A wonderful evocation, entirely pleasurable. I love his play with language and form."

- Suzanne McConnell, author, *Pity the Reader: On Writing With Style by Kurt Vonnegut and Suzanne McConnell*

"Murphy's writing is at turns hilarious and poignant... He understands the pain behind the best jokes."

- Brendan Costello, Jr. *Irish American Writers and Artists*

"Anthony C. Murphy is a gifted storyteller."

- Peter McDermott, *The Irish Echo*

ANTHONY C MURPHY

THE HOUSE OF MURPH

atmosphere press

© 2025 Anthony C Murphy

Published by Atmosphere Press

Cover design by Ronaldo Alves

All images from Anthony C Murphy

No part of this book may be reproduced without permission from the author except in brief quotations and in reviews.

Atmospherepress.com

For Brendan and Jack

Contents

1	Down from the Mountain	1
2	A Load of Rhubarb	3
3	A Tenner to Dennis	5
4	The Firing Squad	8
5	The Day Off	10
6	Proper Cottage	16
7	Tethered as Ghosts	17
8	Gin for Tea	18
9	We're Nuns	20
10	Another Family Plot	23
11	Dad as Roadie	26
12	The Night Fair	28
13	Lancashire Pancakes	30
14	An Echo in the Chancel	33
15	A Heart-Worming Story	35
16	Here's the Rub	38
17	What Held	40

DOWN FROM
THE MOUNTAIN

We three dogs with a Robin Hood complex and one
Blackthorn stick
Hunt blood pudding
Haggis is rarer
But you don't want to know of our
Bow and error
You want to know
What I learned
From Li Po
Bai now

When he came down from the mountain to get drunk with
the butchers
He was no king
He lived up there

I was wondering, though, if Bai Li and William of Occam
Ever discovered each other
So I googled them

I used to have books
And books
But I became
So stupid and bookless
And no
They didn't

Six hundred years apart
That we can straddle
With a look

The wren calls are heard when trapped in a curtain
Silent in the giant maple bough though
And if you listen
You can't hear them
They sing about protein and whine

A LOAD OF RHUBARB

Dad's friend Derek was a keen gardener. He only had a small patch to grow on, like all of us on the estate. My dad had planted potatoes and strawberries, easy stuff to grow. We did have an old poplar tree in the middle of the back garden, though, so we were more limited.

Derek's tastes were tangier. The rhubarb plant is also not so difficult to grow in the tricky climes of the English Northwest, but no one else was trying it on our street. Marrows and carrots, yes, but rhubarb?

Rhubarb crumble was a popular Sunday dessert, with custard, as a matter of course. But no one wanted to eat it more than once a month. And the plant, in all its glorious tumescence, looked like a particularly angry triffid. At least to me and my brothers, in the 1980s, scared out of our wits by *Dr. Who* and the threat of thermonuclear war. We just wanted apples. Or did we?

Derek and my dad were drinking buddies. Derek was a lorry driver and my dad was what you would call a shipping clerk back then. Even though he was qualified in other ways, he wanted a less stressful job, and loved to go out for a pint with the lads. Beer is a great leveler and whiskey a troublemaker, but they knew there was fun to be had in making your own wine.

My dad had tried it over the years—there was a tradition of poteen making back where he grew up. They made it out of potato skins and orange peel, anything. Like the fuel that powers Marty McFly's DeLorean in *Back to the Future*. DeLorean was Irish too, so that would make perfect sense. If he had written the screenplay.

My dad tried his hand at elderberry wine and nettle wine and dandelion wine. All stuff that grew around our house before. I don't know if any of it was any good because we were too young to drink it then. Meanwhile, Derek told my dad that he had made a wine out of bananas that was so strong it "blew a hole in his lavatory". I'm sure that was a line he had picked up in the pub as they were always trying to outdo each other with quotes.

So, between them they decided to use his purple monsters, his man-eating rhubarbs, as an all-new, super strong, blow-your-socks-off vino.

I got all this information out of my dad much later, as I needed to know why they had used me and my brothers as guinea pigs for their evil experiment that late September day.

We were eleven and twelve, and my younger brother was seven. We were innocents, but we were also street kids up for anything. I had smoked roll-ups on the corner and had the occasional shandy beer at Christmas or a wedding champagne, so it wasn't virgin territory. But Derek and my dad needed fresh eyes, or at least an untainted palette, to determine how good their new batch of rhubarb wine really was, because they had been in the pub all afternoon.

My mum must have been in the kitchen, as usual, so they rolled in with a couple of bottles of Derek's TradeMark Rhubarb HomeBrew and gathered us kids in the front room.

It must have tasted okay because we all drank a full glass of the stuff. I liked to think now that it was a murky brew, with bits of flother floating about in it, yet at the same time as delicious as the ambrosia you hear about in, you know, yore.

What was not forgotten by any of us present was the effect it had.

There was dizzy abandon, giddiness, hysteria, and, ultimately, puking, tears, a right old rollicking for my dad, and a never-ever-seen-again Derek.

A TENNER TO DENNIS

Kieran's uncle's dairy farm was in a remote County Kerry village. It took us an all-day trek of double-decker coach, drunken ferry, and one nearly empty train to arrive at our desperation—the hitchhiking in the rain.

We knew we were close, but we weren't getting picked up by tractor today. We would have to get our soggy seventeen-year-old arses to the farm by ourselves.

A saviour in a battered orange car saw our bedraggled state and pulled over.

"Get in, lads!"

We hesitated. I had never been in an orange car before.

"C'mon now!"

It was raining, after all.

I got in the front seat as Kieran needed to lie down in the back.

Dennis, the driver, said he knew the farm we were after. He set off at a furious pace. Kieran had to sit up again.

The windscreen started to rattle; Dennis stuck his thumb on it. He was now driving one-handed, slow to change gear, crawling along the road, cursing all the while.

I could see a crack in the glass slowly spidering upwards from that thumb. The drive took all but ten minutes yet felt a lot longer.

We tried to say thank you and farewell to Dennis as the vibrations in our bodies subsided.

"Three pounds, lads!"

I was confused about the hitchhiking charges. I gave Dennis a fiver and he took it gladly as he one-handedly urged his coughing jalopy into a limp getaway.

We stood there on the farm road, the healthy smell of pure grass-fed cow manure singing in our nostrils. Kieran threw up in the ditch.

We had made it from Manchester to the cow's arse end of this nowhere we wanted to be, this idyll we remembered from younger days, now our escape from modern life.

Kieran's uncle, Christy, fed us sausage sandwiches and made up two beds. I got the feeling he wasn't glad of the company, but he was nice enough. He'd always be busy with his cows anyway, Kieran said. His Friesians, his two collies, Young Joe and Old Joe. There were magpies out of the window. My memories are black and white, even though it was 1989.

During the day, Kieran and I wandered the fields. It was a vast, empty land to us, devoid of the tower blocks and folks we were used to, but not a land that was wasted. Cows munched, streams flowed, wildflowers hugged bees, and long-forgotten trees had peated.

We ate only bread and meat every day and, in the evening, by the fireplace, drank copious amounts of stout at the only pub with the cousins. There was no music except for conversation. There were few books and no television. And the only bus out was on a Tuesday. Bliss. But...

I was useless here. What was I doing? This was the land that time shrugged about when asked what it forgot.

After five nights, I told a sleepy, hungover Kieran that I had to leave. I needed some streetlights and some hubbub or female company, even a vegetable maybe. I wasn't ready for this simplicity.

Christy was up in the field with the dogs, so I sidled off to the pub and asked for Dennis, as it turned out that Dennis was *the* taxi. He said he'd be there soon, and true to his word, he wasn't.

I only waited an hour or so though.

And then we had two pints each.

"What are you going to do, lad? When you get back," Dennis asked me.

"I don't know. Maybe I'll become famous." We took our last draught.

"I hear the computers are the thing," he said wisely.

He knew there was only one train that day. He knew there was no rush to escape that place. The place that doesn't exist anymore. But I was young and had to. I paid him with my last tenner. No tip. No change.

THE FIRING SQUAD

By the age of sixteen, I'd already had three paying jobs and, before that, many voluntary ones. I was a Boy Scout, an altar boy. I served, although I didn't get shot or suffer in any way. There were some twitchy incidents, but I wasn't crawling up chimneys like a Dickensian urchin. I was avoiding flashers as I delivered early-morning newspapers to a prison and collected money for a cancer charity from travelers, at night, in the rain. It was always raining. And I was always outside and soaked. I thought it was what I was supposed to do. I thought everybody had to.

When I got my Saturday job at Tesco, it was lovely. A glowing, warm, friendly place. It had everything you could ever need under one big red roof, for thirteen quid a day.

I sat through some projected History of the Organization. A movie, to me. Mr. Tesco! Wow. It's just your version of Walmart, without the guns. Who is Mr. Walmart?

There is a history but it's not a good one. It's not the Co-Op.

The Co-Operative movement started in Toad Lane, Rochdale, Lancashire, in the 1860s. Born out of a need for workers to take some power back from The Industry that was all-consuming. To put it simply, the workers needed affordable food. So, they started up their own shop. But it became much more than that, worldwide. An ongoing network of neighborliness and community. There's even a village in Queens, New York, called Rochdale. Because it's a Co-Op.

I grew up in Rochdale, Lancashire, in the 1970s and was aware and proud of the Co-Op's history and social impact by the time I was working at Tesco, with its glamorous Christmas, boy band (much anticipated by the masses) TV commercials.

I, however, needed beer, fag money, and, according to my dad, some contribution even though I was still in school, or I would be out on my ear. He couldn't afford my expensive tastes.

So, I went to work for Tesco. Capitalism, folks! It's necessary even for socialists, and sometimes comfy. What the hell, I wasn't about to put fellow workers down and climb up on their shoulders. I was happy to be a cog. Plus, Thatcher was destroying all our unions and I felt more like a be-er than a do-er.

The shop floor manager, Mr. Barker, had thick spectacles and a combover hairstyle. He had been a policeman, apparently. He told me that I should go down to Children's and count all the socks that were hanging on the racks. And to make sure that they were all in pairs. For eight hours.

There were some slight interactions with customers, but I didn't feel able to be a total Tesco ambassador, so I guess I came across as grumpy. Maybe there was a complaint or two.

That was a day.

I ran cross-country in those days, at school, and I found my brain telling me things that I could not stop. Counting socks. Counting socks.

I bought four beers and ate some potato waffles and sausages and went to sleep. My dad was in the pub and my older brother was doing his thing. I wondered if people did this for a life. But then I went to school for a week.

The next Saturday, I woke up late. The thirteen quid from my wage packet the previous week was behind the bar in a pub called The Baum, which is still squatting on Toad Lane in Rochdale. This is next door to the birthplace of The Co-Operative movement. I did make it to Tesco the week after but was told that, seeing as I liked my Saturdays off, I could have them all from now on. I was so grateful I threw up.

I thanked Mr. Barker and tried to live up to his recommendation. It hasn't always been possible.

THE DAY OFF

Inside the white terraced front of The Entwistle Arms, I sit at the bar finishing a pint of Thwaites' Best Bitter. The place is carpeted and wallpapered just like any granny's front parlour—knickknacks and keepsakes and brass pots, family portraits everywhere.

I ask Big Dave, the landlord, for another pint of distraction from the ordinariness. I am seventeen but Dave knows my dad, and it is the 1980s, so I can drink here.

Big Dave sits on one arse cheek, a stray leg a-dangle from his high wooden chair, as he goes over the form in the *Racing Post*.

My dad and his best mucker and drinking buddy, Errol Flynn—no, not that one—are playing darts in the pool room.

We are the only patrons, having started early this Saturday. I have Lucy, our lazy bulldog, dozing at my feet. She's tired out after her sodden and failed rat-catching exploits by the brook, then a compensatory bag of pork scratchings.

What a day!

The day, this capsule, has a numb beauty to it, distilled by the quietude of no one and nowhere to be. It makes me sigh, internally at least, not being one for outward displays of emotion. But I am full of love for all man- and womankind, my neighbour—my distant, at least arm's length, muted neighbour—Manandwomankind.

I could swoon, but I don't want to miss this moment. I am present. There is a fire inside and a torrent out. There's a peace that is sought, bought, or fought for, and only sometimes attained. There is comfort and nourishment right here and now. The turmoil is elsewhere for once. I drink another draught.

Oh, my lord, I love the day off.

"Do you want a game, lad?" Errol punctures my reverie with a dart.

No. I can't handle the competitiveness. They join me instead.

"A pint of diesel, Dave!" my dad orders. And they pick each other's brains over the Newmarket meeting.

"I hear you got arrested again?" I say to Errol. He is older than my dad, a big man with a big grey moustache and a big nose to go with it, or vice versa. He stands tall, always.

"Oh, that weren't nowt," he says, popping peanuts into his mouth. "They always think I'm taking the piss until they see my passport. It's like that song, 'A Boy Named Sue.'"

"You could change your name?" I suggest.

"Who does that but rich folk? Anyway, I'm used to it."

It's a good job his parents weren't called Hitler, I think. They would have had fun with that one.

My dad has one ear on the conversation. "You don't know what his middle name is!"

"Stop that, Joe!" Errol says to my dad. "Leave it!"

Two women walk in then, under the cover of one umbrella. They shake by the doormat, divest raingear, and primp their perms. They are wearing uniforms. I wonder if they had a half-day Saturday down at some factory. One of them stands as tall as Errol. My dad glances in their direction but doesn't give anything away. He orders two halves of lager for them.

"There you go, Sharon."

"Hello, Joe!"

"Nice weather for ducks," Dad says, raising his glass in a toast.

"And thirsty fish!" Errol joins in.

I decide to join as well, trying to think of something that loves water. "And the rabid!" I say, failing.

They all laugh anyway and toast to rabbits.

I am introduced to Sharon and Louise. "This is my son, Sean. These girls work at Buckley Hall."

'Nice to meet yous!' follow. I am emboldened by ale and

attempt to chat up the ladies.

"I used to deliver your newspapers," is all I can manage. It's true I did have a paper round that involved dropping off the weekend news to Her Majesty's Detention Center at Buckley Hall, but it's hardly enamouring, and just points out how young I am.

Still, Sharon and Louise are kind enough to laugh, then leave to find themselves by the fire.

Errol tousles my hair. "You little charmer!"

My dad says, "That Sharon, she's long enough to be continued."

Errol laughs at the so-called banter and then the fellas turn their attention to the more important business of fifty-pence accumulators.

At ten to three, last orders ring.

The place had filled a little, but we had our bubble at the bar that the bit part players had entered for a brief howd'ya-do moment before drifting offstage, and now we are the last left again. Dave kicks us out as he needs a nap. I am feeling that way.

Lucy waters the corner and we amble the five minutes home in the drizzle.

The gas fire is on three bars and the racing comes on the telly. I consider watching the scores coming in, but I fall dozy on the couch. Thoughts of my one-time girlfriend, Deidre, bamboozle my beery brain and I wonder if I'll see her again. I drift into some twitchy dream of her touches.

* * * * *

After an hour and a half or so, I wake. The results are due, and my dad is checking his pools coupon. Errol has been home and came back with some of his home-made wine.

I make myself some toast and watch the scores on the viddy printer. It's a dire day for them. No one has won, no one

I follow. That's the way, I think. When your life is going okay, someone else must suffer and it's usually your team. Or maybe it's just because I'm not wearing my lucky socks.

Dad screws up his coupon and throws it at the telly.

"I don't know why you bother," Errol says.

"You never know," is the wise reply.

"Fancy a glass?" Errol offers his wine.

"Wait!" Dad says. "I have something... From the old sod and the Auld Sod."

He had just got back from Ireland after the sale of the house he grew up in. It had taken five years to sell after my grandad, the old sod, had died and there wasn't any money left. He hadn't shown me what he'd brought back yet, but I had been busy working.

Dad comes back in with a big, clanking box from which he produces a bottle of clear liquid.

"A rascal I met in Desmond's bar gave me this!" Joe says.

"Poteen?" Errol asks.

"Yeh!" He always sucked that word in like a Corker. Like the *yes* as an intake of breath, almost a negation of the positive. "I didn't bring much back, just this and some medals and photos."

"What medals?" I ask, but they are busy testing the moonshine. They give me a nip.

"Tastes like orange," Errol says.

"What medals?" I ask again.

"Oh, yeah. Look at this." My dad hands me an old photograph. It is sepia-tinted with some of the image worn away by time or neglect, but still, a life. There's a group of military men all lined up in rows, like a hirsute football team, unsmiling, buttoned up, dapper and proud.

"That's your Grandad," he says, pointing to the white man front and center, the one surrounded by East Indians wearing dastar turbans and puttees and British Army regulation boots.

"He was an army cook in World War One. In Belgium maybe. These guys must have been his kitchen wallahs."

"I don't think so, Dad. These guys were Sikhs. They were on the front line. Proper soldiers." I pass the photo to Errol. I knew the history of the Raj from school.

"He's right," says Errol. "It could be Turkey or even further east. The English officers probably just lumped the Irish and the Indians together as third class. He never told you what he got up to back then?" Errol asks.

"He never spoke about that bit. But I know he was proud." My dad hands me two medals from the box. "Here."

The medals are basic service medals with an engraving that commends the being of Private Dennis Murphy. I'm guessing that he was.

"There was a lot of that—no talking about it. When he came home from the war, Ireland was a different country, nearly its own country, and he was treated like a traitor by some, especially his brother. Cork was the rebel county, after all. But some went into the British army just to get away from poverty. They didn't care for politics."

"But the whole world changed then," says Errol. "Those Indian guys were fighting the British too—back home, I mean."

"You never saw these before?" I ask my dad about the medals.

"No. No, but I knew he was proud because why else would he set up a Scout troop in Bandon? What he saw out there he tried to do something with the kids of our town..."

I didn't know about that. I was in the Scouts, and it just seemed like a load of messing about, even with a uniform on.

"When did you come over, Joe?" Errol asks.

"1967."

"Did you keep in touch?"

None of us had a phone and letters only came from his sister; I knew that.

"I saw him twice after," Dad says. He looks at me as he says it, and I wonder if he thinks about the day, the one where—or is it when? —he will never see me ever again. It will come. It will all be over. For him, anyway, is what I'm thinking. And he knows it. He has already told me that the waiting can be delicious. I think about burying him then, first, before me, I mean. He saw me in the hospital when I attempted suicide with my friend's mum's depression pills. How he laughed at me then, said I should take my time and enjoy killing myself as we all die anyway, in the end. The end, wait for it.

Then a lull.

And my thoughts turn towards a real pint of beer again.

It's getting to that time when Big Dave will rouse himself and the doors of the pub will swing in the right direction.

"Come on! Let's get to the chippy!" says Errol Flynn. "Gravy!"

PROPER COTTAGE

Next door lived two old brothers
Their interior was decorated with dead skin
Years of it
Dust and dandruff
And dander from Ginger the old dog too
The place had never heard of a vacuum
There was silence in that regard

Nicotine on the ceiling
And ash on the stubbed-out, footworn carpets

We used to knock on their door
As Boy Scouts asking for fifty pence
To do any odd jobs for them
Once a year
But they never told us to clean anything
Just walk Ginger
Or go to the corner shop for the evening paper

I saw Ginger die one day
Knocked down on the street by a car
Not long after, Tara, our cat, moved in with them
They must have been secretly feeding her
Until she filled that hole
As Tara wouldn't come home anymore
Or even say hello

TETHERED AS GHOSTS

Last night I dreamt that I met McConville again
He looked about the same
And yet I wondered if he was dead
Because why should we meet now in my head or his
It's been thirty years and the last time I saw him
After that fight in The Flying Horse Tavern
Where none of us were really damaged
Was because he'd asked for my help
Maybe I just dreamt last night
Made all that up
But his past dad knew my past dad
And they both did
Under similar circumstances pass
And I have not been feeling well
So I wonder now how McConville is
Or if he is anymore
Or am I

GIN FOR TEA

In North Manchester General Hospital, I lost something I could never find again. No, not my appendix—that was at home in a dusty jar.

I wasn't even ill. I was seventeen and had been suffering only from a primal urgency these last few wasted months.

The year before, I had gotten the braces off my teeth and had stopped wearing those thick NHS spectacles.

Strangely, my senses had become more attuned. There was the music, the clothes, the hair, the desire. I wanted to become a part of whatever was going on—to get abandoned to it, though I was confused as to what the 'it' was.

There was a rock group that had informed my life for the last year. I knew their songs upside down. I could never understand how to adopt their cool, that mystery, but I knew it had something to do with black, sunglasses, and too-tight jeans.

My hair was a mess, so that was easy. I didn't have all the gear, though. My jobs delivering newspapers to prison wardens and stacking shelves wouldn't get me far.

The band wasn't glam, more shambolic, so I found an old leather jacket and made do with a tieless school uniform. I had to forego the sunglasses because wearing those in this drizzly town got you beaten up.

Then I found out the band was touring the country. I managed to get a ticket.

On the night of the gig, I got an early train to Manchester. It was all new to me. The place was nearly empty, so I bought a pint with a pub regular's confidence and sauntered to the front to watch the support act that no one liked.

As I rested on the barrier, waiting for my heroes, an arm touched mine and...stayed there. I didn't move even though a shock went through me like I was plugged into the amps myself. Then the arm made movements like it liked being there, and maybe wanted more movements. My arm involuntarily agreed. I hadn't looked over, but I thought we knew who we were enough, being where we were. In our peripheries, our fingers started a dance until we held hands.

As soon as the lights went out, the dry ice came up, and the strobes began, we turned and found each other's mouths.

Drums kicked in and the feedback squealed as the surge of the crowd squeezed us out from the front, pushing us backwards as our grip left the stage—yet we held on to each other. Through the sweaty formless joyous others, we steadily lost our place, but we hung on, lip-locked, and became a tango in the middle of the straggled pogoing circle.

We were oblivious to the show now, familiar songs washing over us as we ended up out of it, breathless at the back of the room.

That band back then rarely lasted longer than twenty-nine minutes on stage before a fight broke out. It's not why I was there, or why I wanted to leave. I loved them; I could listen to their songs anytime. So, we did leave, and they wouldn't care.

She took me to her room in the hospital. No, she wasn't an escapee—she was a trainee, Nurse Andrea, nineteen years old.

That night, I discovered what all my preening and longing was for. What the mystery was. And my urgency abated.

I only had brothers, so some of it was a shock.

Menstruation hadn't been covered in biology class by our teacher, the terse and blustery Sister Philomena.

"We are blood." Andrea shrugged afterwards. "But, you know, sorry for not saying!"

At least we're in a hospital, I thought.

Was I a man now? Now I had 'it'! ...and yet I had *lost* 'it.'

Unlike this appendix, I guess some parts of you aren't meant to be kept on the shelf.

"WE'RE NUNS!"

I am on a boat full of them. Novices, anyway, is what they tell me. Out of habit.

I haven't had sex for a month. I am thinking, me too. But I was making polite chat when I asked what they all did for a living.

The novices had been noisy and full of themselves, and I was party to it by proximity. It was only our accents that separated us. We were sat on the floor together because the Dublin ferry was so busy that all the seats had been given up to the infirm. It was a choppy crossing.

Nuns? They shut me down with that shocker, so I contented myself with a can of beer. One of them wanted a quieter word, though. She waited for the attention to tangent itself before she isolated me.

"What's the matter?" she asks.

"Not much." I lift the urn and show her. "Ash! No matter really, just my dad."

I'm drunk and she knows.

"He needs an introduction," I say as I pat the urn, to make her feel more included.

"I'm Fiona, pleased to meet you," she says, shaking the urn like a hand.

"This is Joe."

"You going to drink all of those?" She points out the case of Stella I had purchased from the duty-free nestled between my knees.

"Not possible. Would you like one?"

"Nnnnn!" She shakes her head.

I offer what I am cradling to her friends then. "You?"

Her girlfriends seem offended that I've entered into their auras once more, but they take a beer each anyway.

"Don't you think you've had enough?" Fiona says.

"Not yet."

"How would you know?"

"I wouldn't."

"When do you stop?"

"When I do."

"Does it hurt?"

"Doesn't everything?"

"Jesus heals. He's there for you."

I don't know if she's having me on.

"He's there for you," I say.

"For all."

"How would you know?"

"Because he is."

"Just because?"

"Yes," she says.

"I've been godless since I was eight. Have a beer!"

She shakes again.

"We've just come from a choir competition."

"How was that?"

"We won, thanks for asking!"

I see a unity in them, a sureness; they're a big-toothed grin of a team.

"Well done." I drink.

"We're celebrating."

"Doesn't look like it," I say.

"You don't have to get...listen... Come with me."

So I go with her—I have to take my dad—up the carpeted stair onto the top deck. She holds the urn whilst I pull at the wind-stuck, leaden door. We look out for a while. The whole world is dark silver. Then, there, in the howl, and staring at the waves in the dark, she kisses me. I don't know why.

"Where are you going?" Fiona asks me, even as I stand there.
"I'm taking him back."
"Home." She flexes her neck.
"Yes." I put the urn down between my feet so that I can free my hands.

She kisses me more. It's a big snog.

We promise each other some more sunrises as we see the land we look for. She glows in the beauty of the morning. It must feel good to be going home, to belong. It's my first time here in years. I suddenly feel like a tourist in a familiar place that has grown without me. I break away from her and apologise.

We just stand there, in our own wake. It's awkward. She starts to shift from foot to foot after a while.

"It was nice meeting you."

"It was nice meeting you."

She goes back down to find her coven as we dock.

I give everyone some space, the last on deck again. When I descend, it is through some squegging emotions. I know that they weren't nuns, and that they've drunk all my beer. My dad rolls about the ship in his new plastic house, laughing his lid off.

ANOTHER FAMILY PLOT

"So?" the barmaid asks.

"A pint of that." I point and dig coins from my pockets.

"What's up?"

"I lost my dad." I sigh.

"Uh huh!" She's listening. "Have you phoned anyone?"

"It's not like that. He was in an urn," I say. "My bag was stolen. I was at a party."

"Well. Okay... Where did you last see him?" she asks, matter-of-factly.

"Dublin," I say.

And she laughs. She snorts a big one and curses and crosses herself to keep the demons at bay. "Holy feckin' Jeezus! Do you even know where ye are?"

"No," I say.

"Well, I hope you said your goodbyes!" she says and tuts at me.

"Yeah," I say. "Not really. I just brought the ashes from England to get buried back home in Cork."

"Here," she says, handing me a pint. "You're in Wicklow now." She shakes her head.

"Thanks!" I do remember the train, vaguely.

The stout burns my throat, but I don't care. I wonder if this has happened before. The stealing of an urn! It must have happened before. Maybe they thought there was something valuable in it?

I sit there sipping and feeling sorry for myself. A few more patrons enter the pub and are familiar with me. Sharon lights a fag and blows the smoke out of the side of her mouth and picks a piece of tobacco out of her teeth, I guess—it could be something else.

"So, what are you going to do?"

"Can I get one of those?" I ask, pointing to her cigarette.

"No." She considers. "You have to earn it."

I am feeling hungry now with my emptied belly. I look about the bar but they don't have much. "Can I have a pickled egg, please?"

"Sure," says Sharon. "It's your funeral... Sorry!"

"I like them," I say. I tuck into it, and it's like a chemistry lesson exploding in my mouth, but it helps with my reality, gives me a jolt. "Will you let me collect glasses for you tonight?" I ask, cheeks full of acidic protein. "Then I can earn it."

Sharon thinks. "Why not?" She puffs. "But I tell you, it's quiet on Mondays."

She gives me one of her cigarettes. I agree with her but I have a lot going on. I have to get to Cork for the funeral service. And I have no remains to bury. *Where are you, Dad?* My head is clear as a hangover. I check my socks for cash.

"Sharon, can I have the whole jar of eggs, please? And another pint."

"Where are you going with this?" she asks, but she gives me the jar. The weight and size of it are comparable to the urn. Of course, it's glass and not plastic—I'll have to explain something to my Aunt Maureen, but not that I haven't got my dad with me... And there are only ten eggs left.

"It's doable!" I say to Sharon.

"Sure. Weirdo!" she says.

"Okay, everyone, the pickled eggs are on me! Do it for the old feller!" I shout and raise the jar aloft with both hands like I've just won the cup. I hear one whoop and I have a few takers but...I have to eat most of the eggs myself. It's a chastening experience. I know I can throw them away, but that's such a waste! I probably won't eat for a while anyway. My stomach revolts a little, but I manage.

All night I collect empties for my new friends and clean out the ashtrays. I stash all of their fag ash in the old pickle jar.

Later, I have to sift it a little, but at least I have a new dad, although he's lost weight. He smells of vinegar and old smoke, but he would anyway. I tighten the lid on him.

DAD AS ROADIE

I can't remember how many gigs you boys had done those last two weeks, but we were now heading as far east in Europe as was booked. You had played Dresden, I remember liking, and now, after Prague, we kept moving.

It was dark, early morning, December, the motorway was clear. You guys fell asleep in the back of the van immediately after the gig. Sometimes there's no *after*party. We had been travelling constantly, eating, sleeping in situ, no hotels for the last few days. You were all knackered. All I had to do was get you to Poland.

There was only one bunk in the van and you took it in turns. This time, Sam was sitting behind me.

The snow came down towards us. We were not moving forwards and yet I was doing fifty miles per hour. We entered a vortex.

I gunned the van and squinted through the windshield. I wanted to outrun the avalanche. We had to beat the metronome. I couldn't tell if we were coming down off a mountain, though. As I drove forward, I felt like we were going backwards. The snow became horizontal and, no matter how much pressure I put on the accelerator, I was on a blank white page, going nowhere. Except that it looked like we were now doing seventy miles per hour through fresh snow, forging our way east, apparently, but clueless as to where we were in the real world. I couldn't see our progress and there was no way to know if anything was better up ahead. I was guessing.

Some lights there and a service station. I need to blink, so I pull in. You boys are still. I close my eyes after parking up and join you in sleep. Do you know what Europe means? That's what I dream.

When I wake after an hour or two, the snow is worse. We are between nowhere and somewhere, amidst blizzard and hills. I just want to get off the mountain and we have to get to the venue by tomorrow afternoon—today afternoon. I decide to chance it again. I brush the excess snow off the windshield; my hands seize up. You guys are snug and useless. I have to get going. The engine starts, I let it warm, and we pull out, skidding onto the 'autobahn,' and the van immediately turns side-on into the middle of the three lanes.

Like a dog on a trampoline, I brake, halt, hunker down, and wait for the world to stop with me. I was only going fifteen miles per hour and luckily there are no fast-approaching vehicles coming up behind, so, after a still, silent second or two, I manage to rev, turn hard, reverse, and usher the tyres into some kind of groove. I can see forward now, I think, and pump us on. I get up to speed. Maybe we are out of it, towards sea level, because then there is some slush and traction and daylight.

As I get back up to seventy miles per hour and feel confident, the side door of the van opens. A rush of cold air and snow hits the back of my neck. Sam, half-asleep, has decided to go pee. The van swerves with my turn-around-to-look motion, and Sam swerves also. He holds on, though, still semi-comatose, braced at an open door on a motorway, letting it all hang out, as I then tell him, calmly, to please sit down and I will pull over and park. You, the rest of the band, are oblivious to all of this. The cold gusts of Eastern Europe do not wake the wearied Western heads of teenagedom. Sam staggers back into the confines of the van and I brake slowly and stop, managing to close the van door with a side swipe of my gear-free arm and expel just one loud, resigned "Fuck."

THE NIGHT FAIR

Parked all garishly and spread out
Across the town hall car park
Like a many-tentacled thing
With multi-coloured neon bulbs on
And luminous paint onioning off
The whole thing thrilling
And yet up close
It screamed and honked like a dying monster
But they didn't care
They clambered into cars
And restrained themselves in chrome
She was sitting across from him, or vice versa
At an angle, in different vehicles
They looked up
"I know you," she said.
And he said, "Do you?"
"Yes." She laughed. "I guess I don't."
And she whirled away as the ride started
And he spun away too on another ellipse
Their paths crossed intermittently
At sixty miles an hour
Smiles, or grimaces, just a blur of white
A smudge of red
The only constant being the rock-solid soundtrack
As they sped in a waltz
And looked for the familiar
There she is again, there he is
Trying to concentrate on some horizon

As their heads battered by G force and fun
Was it?
Eventually gave in to a weird hysteria
Laughter in a tolerable pain
Then it stopped
And the cars came back to their start
Positioned for take-off
They got out, decarnivaled themselves
And helped each other stand on the ground
What was that all about, they said, is it over?

LANCASHIRE PANCAKES

On Shrove Tuesday, the family all vowed to deny ourselves our own something good until Good Friday. At least that was the plan. You know, just like Jesus had done in the desert. Wear a hair shirt, put Satan behind you, and then be beside yourself with hallucinatory deprivation.

We looked forward to the visions, but before that we had to eat all the flour, eggs, butter, and sugar in the cupboard. We were duty-bound by religion. It was our god-given right to stock up our guts before dealing with the devil.

In England back then, everyone usually ate the pancakes with just lemon juice and a lot of sugar. It became such a thing that lemon juice was sold in little plastic lemons by a company called Jif. We called it Pancake Day, but the telly guys called it Jif Lemon Day.

Me and my school friends wanted to eat as many pancakes as possible. It was a thrice-a-year day for us to get full of pleasure. We discussed it at school like Christmas or Easter—birthdays being of a more personal nature.

"How many pancakes are you gonna eat?"

"Five. I'm gonna have five."

"I'm gonna have seven at least..."

"I'm gonna eat so many I throw up before *Dr. Who*."

None of us knew the meaning of Mardi Gras, but we knew the reason—to get fat.

To us it was just a part of the year, not really a commitment, but definitely a tradition.

Then came the real fast promises. There were variations, but usually it went like this:

My mum was responsible for shopping, cooking, cleaning, then avoiding my dad's amorous advances. She took care of three boys of different ages, a dog, a cat, a budgerigar, and several fish, all called Fred. So, she didn't give up anything. In fact, she got herself some more Walnut Whips, and extra bottles of Blue Nun Reisling now that my dad had said, to himself, and his god, that he would foreswear the drink for forty nights. He had the Catholic guilt thing drummed into him and, by gob, he could stand the challenge. Although we all doubted that and only listened when he shouted. Most years he succeeded in staying out of the pub. He even hid behind the curtain on St. Patrick's Day. All his friends thought he was dead. If they passed him in the street, they'd seen a ghost of himself.

"I'll see you at Easter, boys," was his sly, almost remorseful greeting.

He did well, though, his former self even continuing the practice after their divorce. He was proud of the effort and made promises of a brighter future. I often wonder if he died in February on purpose, dreading the ensuing Lent.

As for the rest of us:

The dog gave up chasing the cat. The cat gave up chasing both the dog and the budgie. The budgie gave up teasing the cat and stopped heckling the dog. The fish gave up life, often.

My older brother gave up masturbating—at least that's what it said in his diary. And he did take his Madonna poster down one year.

My younger brother usually gave up chocolate. Or at least one specific bar of chocolate. Probably Bounty Bars, knowing him, or maybe Twix.

And as for me, I gave up pancakes. Well, we only had them once a year anyway.

I vowed one sickly year never to eat them ever again was what I said.

I make them sometimes now, though, for my daughter. She likes it when I flip them, as I watched my mum and dad do—back in the pan and not on the ceiling, we'd say. And we put sugar and real lemon on, in the nearly old English way. No syrup. And she loves them. But none pass my lips.

AN ECHO IN THE CHANCEL

I was twelve years old but still I knew something more than the old ones when Father Coyne made me scour the pews, to strafe for waywards that Midnight Mass, St. Patrick's Church, Rochdale, Lancashire, 1983.

Father McKeown had absconded, Father Eckersley was too long in the bathroom, so Sausage-Head Coyne handed me his vestments with pink, shaky fingers as he urged me on to lock up.

There was a massive Byzantine mosaic mural behind the altar that glistered even in the dark. Matthew, Mark, Luke, and John. Dead, judging eyes staring down on us, on me. All-knowing. It was awesome in a bad way. Like they were waiting to be reanimated. I had seen some *Sinbad* films, and *Jason and the Argonauts*. I had fretful dreams of being squished between giants' digits.

The whole place still smelt of incense. It made me want to genuflect, but that was the point, I guess. They wanted us to bow and scrape whilst they sipped and scarfed the coffers. Of course I think this now. Back then I was as petrified as the marble altar and always in some kind of reverie brought on by all the gold, frankincense, and stunning internal murmurs of that nonexistent god frightening the bejeesus out of my every slumbering moment. Did I believe in any of this nonsense? It was all real, though. I was here. If other people believed, there must be something.

Then I heard the cough.

"Hello?" I said.

There was no answer. There was no echo in the chancel, not an aural one anyway. There was just a man asleep on the cold stone ground.

"Hello?" I said again to the sleeping tramp. But as I got nearer, I realized that it was a man I had seen before, somewhere, everywhere. A man I had maybe mentioned before.

This man had big ears, a big nose, and was wearing tweeds. It was Himself.

I had a rush of knowing, and then, weirdly, a sadness. Or a sad weirdness. I knew who he was. It was Himself! But I didn't know. I had seen him before, a lot. My memories spooled in my brain. I wasn't me then; I was younger. I was with my dad. My dad knew this man too, back then. He had seen him, he said, everywhere he had ever lived. In Wolverhampton and Balham and Kearsley and even back home in Bandon. We had forgotten Himself until he just turned up again. He was easy to recognize. Why did we forget? What did he want? He never spoke. He just was. He was some kind of portent. My dad said that Himself could be his ugly guardian angel.

I would only ever talk about Himself to my dad, because he was the only other one to see. But that was then.

All this came like a wave into my being as the big-eared, tweed-wearing enigma raised himself from his slab stone pillow and grinned at me. In that smile, and through those watery eyes, I knew that he knew everything about me. A panic thumped within me; I could hardly breathe. Himself just grinned and made a slight whiny "eeeeh!" sound as drool slid from the corner of his mouth and dangled on a saliva string towards the marble floor. I watched it and froze, but Himself stayed put also. I had to go. All I knew was that I had to leave. I ran from that place, never to go back. I hung up my cassock that night. And thankfully Christmas Day took away the night terrors.

After I grew up and after my dad died, I never saw the tramp again. But once a year, I remember, and I am still waiting over here, in America, for an echo of Himself to appear.

A HEART-WORMING STORY

When my dad said that he was 'going to see a man about a horse,' we knew he was off to the bookies and then the pub to watch the races. It was that Irish code that has been recounted by many a thirstily desperate man to escape from the noise of the wee brawling bawlers and the looks of the scowling missuses. And how we didn't miss his aroma when he went. But there was a bit of mystery as to what he got up to.

Sometimes it would be 'I'm off to see a man about a dog,' and surprises appeared on our doorstep occasionally.

Ben didn't last long. He was some kind of black lab mix but had awful distemper. If he had been a car, he would have been as lemon as the shite on our screaming mother's carpet. Mindy was next. Me and my brother were in love with her, and got to name her after Pam Dawber, but Mindy was moved on to a neighbour as quick as you can say 'Shazbot!' My mum's only refuge was the kitchen, and my dad's thoughts of no dinner meant that these untrained strays had to go.

A year later, my dad tried again. By this time, we had a goldfish, a budgie, and a cat. Housebound, captive nature! But my dad yearned for a companion to accompany him on his jaunts to the bookies and the pub. He needed a weekend familiar.

So, Toby arrived one day. He was a Cairn terrier mix but looked like a West Highland with long legs. He was fluffy and cute (to look at) and no trouble in the kitchen. And he was kind of small, so my mum tolerated him. He wasn't a lap dog, though—he had no need to be patted, petted, stroked, or cuddled. He was a fierce hunter that craved only meat, and sometimes tyres. He got on with the cat okay; after just one fight he thought better of her. But even the cat knew that when it was dinnertime, we all stayed away from Toby's bowl.

There was something about owning a semi-feral animal that my dad was proud of. Not that Dad had captured this particular beast himself. But Toby only listened to my dad. And if Toby ever deferred, the dog would have seven kinds of dandruff kicked out of him or sometimes suffer the lash. With no biscuit.

Still, me and my brother enjoyed Toby's company when we were out. Back in those days, on the estate, everyone let their dogs loose. The dogs had to skulk, fight, or submit—they had to prove themselves all the time. They never formed a pack, because all had homes to go to when it got dark.

Toby was a keen hunter. We took him over to the field at Heybrook and he would catch voles and rats before we had even seen a movement in the grass. He would jump in the stream and swim to their nests, shake them to death, and throw them at our feet. He loved to swim and he loved to eat, but more than anything he loved the chase. He was as fast as a Scalextric slot car with brand-new batteries. A streak of dirty white lightning.

One time, he chased a bus all the way down Yorkshire Street, angry at the big rubber wheels for some reason. I ran after him, screaming, but my voice had none of my dad's menace yet, so Toby was oblivious. I was desperate for Toby to stop and just come home with me before we got all the way into the town center, and all the people there. He got bored when he realized, at a bus stop, after a frenzied, snarling attempt, that he couldn't pop the fecking thing, and I managed to pick him up and tuck him under my arm to then trudge the mile back home, avoiding all eye contact. Thankfully there weren't many cyclists round our way back then, but kids who got Christmas BMXs were very wary of Toby.

And then one day Toby was gone. My mum had had enough of his petulance. We didn't know where he went but a *suitable* home was mentioned. My dad didn't own a gun, so that was out of the question. He had given in. The budgie had died, and the goldfish. The cat was still around, though. Although the cat moved next door after my mum left us all a year later.

My dad moved to a town in the foothills of the Pennines on the Lancashire side, and eventually found a suitable sidekick. Skittles was a red Collie. Skittles went everywhere with my dad, and they became a feature in the town. It was a small town and pub life wasn't on the agenda anymore. So, the bookies, the library, two butchers, and an off-license owner were the main drag. My mum never owned an animal. They had always been foisted upon her, infiltrating a home life that she was trying to keep clean and tidy. My parents were very different people with nothing shared except their sons. Skittles was a dog who had my dad's eyes, she said. He was a good dog too, but not a good human.

Skittles informed the neighbours, and the bookies, when my dad didn't get out of his chair on his last day. The dog came to the funeral and lived out his life with my younger brother and a cat called Red.

HERE'S THE RUB

Back then, we slept in bunks. Over the years, we took turns as to who slept where. I'm still not comfortable falling asleep near other people, and probably because I never knew where my own bed was supposed to be. It has taken me a long time to settle, and I have slept in weird places sometimes, spending many nights asleep in bags, not plastic ones, in disused buildings, or on buses, in vans, on the street, under bridges, and in a few solitary jail cells that have been more accommodating than my under-the-brother-bunk that one night back then.

We should be fast asleep. It must be a Friday night because my dad was in the pub and my mum hadn't gone out at all. She would do on a Saturday if she was in the mood.

Then there's that vicious boom.

It stuns me and I wonder about my brother, if he's listening too now. But I would like to know more about the other room, so I listen, and he is talking in low rumbles that vibrate the very walls of us, about how he should be doing something more and about fingering and wetness and hardness. I know, I think I know, what that means. My mum is talking in hushed tones, sobbing, Ah! Mum! Crying about her younger sister and what a devil he was to do that to her also when she was so young. What a devil. And urging him to stop and leave her be now and forever. And he won't have it. He won't. Not ever again.

She will have a black eye in the morning, and everyone will know that we lay there in our stupid pyjamas, cowering, wondering why we didn't jump onto his big, freckled back and stop him from hurting her.

Things change after that night and with time the noise becomes muffled. That loud crack that made splinters of us all is now a distant shockwave, ever decreasing.

WHAT HELD

The knock at the door was more of a thud. It sounded low—down, I mean, not on the knocker. And we have a doorbell as well, don't we? I remember thinking. What is the point of that then? Whoever it was couldn't reach, maybe? Some tiny Girl Scout with a cookie delivery?

Luckily, I was in the kitchen, and, in between my heavy-handed crashing of the dishes, I heard the thud on the door. The others of the house were too far indoors for me to start howling at them to answer the blessed thing, so *I* did. Probably muttering that "*I* do everything around here."

I opened the back door and saw no one. I opened the screen door, which still had the glass panel from the winter. I didn't see anyone, but there was a glimpse of red in my periphery. So, I looked down.

There, on the boot-scrubbing welcome mat, was a small bird. A stunned cardinal. It looked up at me, but otherwise just stood there, unafraid, in a daze. At that point, I was just glad it wasn't a raven.

After a second or two of no fight or flight, I reached back in and got my phone to take a photo before it flew away. It blinked and cocked its head, but otherwise it was not inclined to move. I ran in to tell the others of the house, hoping it would stay where it was.

Bella was thrilled to see it; she was always grabbing salamanders and worms and frogs and squeezing other people's pets, but, Oh! a whole live, wild bird was just... "Oh!"

She got a gardening glove on, crouched down, and scooped the bird up, then stood there proud, like a falconer.

The cardinal was still too dizzy to fly, and in that state looked like it was enjoying the experience. Not stoned, but glassed as it was.

So, Bella took it out into the back garden to reacquaint it with the trees and such.

The bird stayed with her, though, unwilling to try for the branches.

We marveled at Bella's ability with animals, sometimes, and said how she would probably become a zookeeper, or a vet, or an unwitting euthanasia specialist for the small things of the planet.

She wanted to keep the bird—of course she did. It was hers now.

I told her to further it up into the peach tree, maybe just sit there for a bit. It was the easiest tree to climb and had places to perch. We took loads of photos and sent them straight to Grandma, who liked them instantly. Thumb!

The bird got some memory back as it tested its wing feathers by flapping but not taking off.

And all this sent me back in time to when I was ten years old.

One hot, rainy day, I was at Heybrook, a small stream that cut through woods and by our housing estate before eventually meeting the River Roche near the town of Rochdale, where I grew up.

I was there with Dad and my brother, Jase, as we walked our dog, Toby. The grass was high and feathery by the banks, and the warmth brought that intoxicating stench from all the straining blossom and steamy earth after a rain.

Toby, the terrier, had just shaken a water rat to death and I had been shaking him to get it out of his jaws when my dad spotted some color in the willow on the opposite bank.

"Give me your kagoul!" he shouted at Jase, and then started into the water. Jase didn't ask why; he handed it over like a relay baton and Dad waded.

The brook was mainly shallow and not fast-flowing, but

there were slick rocks and pools, and I had been submerged once before whilst trying to jump onto an opposite branch.

"What is it?" I asked.

"I'll find out." Dad got across to the other bank and ventured into the nether regions of the weeping tree. Toby was not bothered by this as he had been warned, with a belt, about the water for now, so he ran off after a ball in the field nearby.

You couldn't catch Toby unless he was sodden and weighed down by the river weeds, so we usually let the Rochdale Asian Cricket Alliance deal with him. They needed the fielding exercise and the target practice.

We watched Dad scramble with some intent. Jase, with the weariness of the firstborn, asked me, "Why didn't he take your jacket?"

I shrugged within my comfort.

Dad had told us how he used to catch linnets, his favorite of the songbirds. How he used to tickle trout and catch water hens back in Ireland when he was our age. Here he was still at it.

There was a great rustling and bending of branches. Some of the light green leaves fluttered into the brook like the remnants of a pillow fight. There was a grunt and a few curses and then a splash. Dad waded back over to us, holding my brother's jacket balled up between his hands, which were bleeding from fresh cuts.

"Come on, we have to get it home. Get the fecking dog!"

At home in the kitchen, Dad revealed what he had captured in the now-bloody hood of my brother's rainproof jacket.

It was a cockatiel.

It was a fancy-looking bird, not one usually seen on our street. It was unharmed and fluffed itself. It had mainly white plumage with pink shocked cheeks, a sharp, hooked, snarled beak, and a lovely yellow quiff.

We called it Elvis.

It crapped all over the kitchen—Thank you very much!—to

Mum's exasperation. We let it flap about in there and closed the doors as we went out to the shed.

We put Elvis in Spud the budgie's (RIP) old cage with some cornflakes and water on a sandpaper floor and we cooed and watched. Elvis pranced about, cockily, and started to talk. We were amazed by it; what an amazing bird.

Over the next few days, me and Jase taught Elvis some new words. We got him to say "Toby!" which drove the dog mad. Toby would be running in and out of the kitchen, knocking my mum over and treading on my dad, who smacked me on the head and called me a smart arse for ever thinking of it.

We did scout the neighborhood and asked if the bird belonged to anyone around or if anyone had an aviary, but no one claimed to know.

Elvis could have flapped from miles away and just got tired.

Dad wasn't allowed to keep his pets for very long, though.

Elvis got sold to another label after two weeks. Toby went the same way after a while. And then so did Mum.

Nothing lasts forever is a truism—or a get-out.

I was the last to leave that town.

Oh yes. Back to the future present.

The cardinal took about an hour to regain all of its abilities. After two small, aborted flights, the bird managed to gain enough height to get going. And it flew away like the World War One Red Baron ace, listing slightly after a dogfight.

Bella never even had time to name it, but there are plenty more birds in the tree.

Though we think this one comes back. We think, as Northern Cardinals are quite territorial, it's probably the same one, back from whatever wars he's been fighting. They must have good memories too.

About Atmosphere Press

Founded in 2015, Atmosphere Press was built on the principles of Honesty, Transparency, Professionalism, Kindness, and Making Your Book Awesome. As an ethical and author-friendly hybrid press, we stay true to that founding mission today.

If you're a reader, enter our giveaway for a free book here:

SCAN TO ENTER
BOOK GIVEAWAY

If you're a writer, submit your manuscript for consideration here:

SCAN TO SUBMIT
MANUSCRIPT

And always feel free to visit Atmosphere Press and our authors online at atmospherepress.com. See you there soon!

About the Author

ANTHONY C MURPHY grew up in Lancashire, England. He worked as a postman for fourteen years, toured Europe as a road manager, and has been an associate producer of live poetry nights and open mics. He has performed at spoken word events in the UK and the US for the last twenty years. He has published a novel, *SHIFTLESS*, available through Atmosphere Press, and is a member of Irish American Writers and Artists, NYC.

He currently lives in North Westchester, NY.

www.ingramcontent.com/pod-product-compliance
Lightning Source LLC
LaVergne TN
LVHW041638070526
838199LV00052B/3428